This edition published in 1999 by SMITHMARK Publishers,
a division of U.S. Media Holdings, Inc., 115 West 18th Street, New York, NY 10011.

SMITHMARK books are available for bulk purchase for sales promotion and premium use.
For details write or call the manager of special sales, SMITHMARK Publishers, 115 West 18th Street, New York, NY 10011, (212) 519-1300.

Cat Hiss-tory
was produced by Lionheart Books, Ltd.,
5105 Peachtree Industrial Blvd., Atlanta, Georgia 30341

Design: Carley Wilson Brown

ISBN: 0-7651-1052-0

Printed in Hong Kong

10 9 8 7 6 5 4 3 2 1

Library of Congress Cataloging-in-Publication Data

Bell, Bill.
    Cat hiss-tory : a feline tour through the ages / illustrated by
Bill Bell ; text by Frederica Templeton.
        p.   cm.
    Summary: A humorous illustrated survey of the role of cats in
world hiss-tory.
    ISBN 0-7651-1052-0 (alk. paper)
    1. Cats--Caricatures and cartoons--Juvenile literature.
2. American wit and humor, Pictorial--Juvenile literature. 3. Cats-
-Juvenile humor. [1. World history--Wit and humor. 2. Cats--Wit
and humor.]   I. Templeton, Frederica.   II. Title.   III. Title: Cat
    history.
    NC1429.B3552A4   1999
    741.5'973--dc21
                                                    98-46694
                                                        CIP
                                                        AC

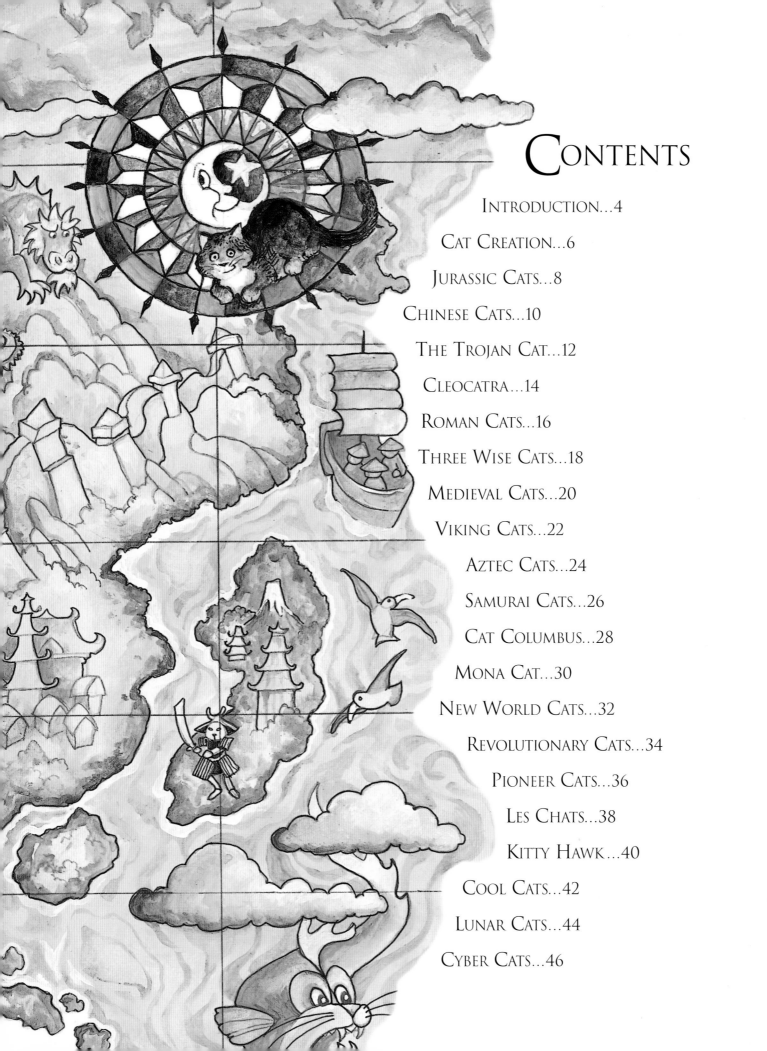

CONTENTS

INTRODUCTION

AFTER many years of study and deep, deep thinking, I have come to the conclusion that the world is divided into only two types of creatures: dogs and cats. If you consider this for a moment, you will see the truth of it. Dogs approach life with an indiscriminate appetite and an unquestioning acceptance of things as they are. They are lively, loud, and loving. Cats, on the other hand, are extremely discreet and never accept things at face value. They are self-possessed, silent, and selective. It is my contention that based on these differences the most important, pivotal moments in history have always been determined by the unique qualities of cats. In my long career I have often pondered the immortal words of Oliver Catwell Holmes, "Hiss-tory is painting a picture, not doing a sum." When I was asked to put together a collection of my favorite moments in hiss-tory, it seemed a perfect opportunity to heed this advice. And so, dear reader, I offer you this illustrated tour of cats through the ages with the sincere hope that you will find it entertaining as well as, dare I say, illuminating. Join me for a decidedly personal look at cats in hiss-tory.

—PHINEAS T. TIGER

Bill Bell

CAT CREATION

IN THE BEGINNING the Great One said,
"Let there be cats!" and so there were cats. And the
Great One said, "Be fruitful and multiply!" and the
cats obeyed so that the earth was soon filled with
cats of infinite variety. And the Great One said,
"Obey me and you shall have all that you desire."
But the cats were not impressed. They disdained
this magnificent offer in favor of nine lives of self-
determination. And so it is that through
the ages cats have obeyed no one.

JURASSIC CATS

IN THE PREDAWN of hiss-tory we find the first glimmerings of the imaginative spirit. Though our earliest ancestors were wily and ferocious hunters, once the needs of food and shelter were met, they turned their attention to the pleasures of ornamentation and invention. Evidence of their superior powers of observation can still be found on the walls of the spacious, dry caves they inhabited so long ago. With charcoal from spent fires and pigments from the earth, Jurassic cats made the first known drawings, mainly of themselves. Also, to have a new toy to play with, they invented the wheel.

CHINESE CATS

AFTER too many years of being harassed from the north by hordes of invading barbarian cats, the Chinese cats decided to build a wall. This wall was to be of such monumental proportion and strength that the Chinese cats would never again have to worry about their uncivilized neighbors. From simple mounds of dirt to elaborate stone towers, the wall took shape over thousands of years. Millions of cats came from all over China to build the fortification and many gave several of their lives to it. For 1,500 miles it meownders its way from the Yellow Sea north of present day Beijing westward along the southern edge of the Mongolian Plain.

Alas, it proved ineffective and the Chinese cats took up political theory.

11

Trojan Cats

IN THEIR MONUMENTAL effort to recapture Helen, the fairest feline of them all, the Greek cats had besieged Troy for nine fruitless years. Finally deciding that superior brains were needed to break the impasse, they laid down their arms and picked up their hammers to construct what they knew the Trojans could never resist: a large wooden cat. Within the hollow center they placed a dozen of their best warriors and then they pretended to leave the field of battle. Ignoring the warnings of Catsandra, who begged her fellow citizens to beware of Greek-built cats, the curious Trojans pulled the intriguing artifact within the impregnable walls of Troy. In the dead of night, the warriors crept out and opened the gates of Troy to the waiting Greeks. The deception was successful, Troy was reduced to dust, and the beautiful Helen was restored to the red-haired cat, Menelaus.

CLEOCATRA

ANCIENT EGYPT was a catocracy, so it is not surprising that one of their most famous rulers was Queen Cleocatra. Noted for her exquisite beauty, she also possessed wry cunning. She thwarted efforts by her brother and co-ruler to steal the throne of Egypt by seeking the help of the top Roman tom, Julius Caesar. Outsmarting her enemies, she had herself delivered to Caesar rolled up in a Persian rug. The Roman general found her captivating. He instantly fell in love with her, restored her to her throne, and took her back to Rome where she lived with him until his unfortunate assassination. Like the wise and clever feline she was, she soon after allied herself with another powerful Roman, Mark Catony. He also found her irresistible. Together they defied the forces of Rome only to fail, tragically and romantically. Catony, believing a false report that she had been killed during the Battle of Actium, took his own life. When the news reached the ill-fated and very much alive queen, she chose to follow his example. Legend has it that it was the bite of an asp that stilled her breath, but I have it on authority that she died of a broken heart.

ROMAN CATS

ROME wasn't built in a day, it's true, but it took a surprisingly short time for a once small town on the banks of the Tiber to become a very large empire. Once they had finished subjugating barbarian tribes, Roman cats spent their time building marble temples and basilicas and getting together for fun and games. The Colosseum, that great and lasting monument to public entertainment, dates from 80 A.D. Within its walls ferocious paw-to-paw contests, death-defying chariot races, and fabulous festival marches thrilled the local citizenry. The mighty empire was eventually undone by that feline Achilles heel—vanity. The emperors came to consider themselves gods—as did many of the ordinary citizen cats. One emperor, Nero, played his fiddle as the city burned; his subjects groomed themselves and took naps.

THREE WISE CATS

IN THE ANCIENT world soothsayers who followed the teachings of Zoroaster were called

magi (from which we get our word magic). Practitioners of astrology, they scanned the heavens in

search of omens, seeking to find in the configuration of the twinkling lights some answers to the

mysteries of life. Three such wise cats—Balthasar, Melchior, and Casper—believed they had found

such an omen in one brilliant star, which they followed to the town of Bethlehem in Judea. Their precious gifts of gold, frankincense, and myrrh did seem a trifle out of place in the stable they visited, but they were not disappointed. They found the simplest, yet most comprehensive answer of all: "Peace on earth, good will to men."

MEDIEVAL CATS

DURING the 500 or so years that we now call the Feudal Epoch, fierce battles over territory kept most felines terribly busy. Fiefdoms dotted the landscape like mushrooms and every cat was king of his castle. But life in the Middle Ages was not confined to the clash of swords and the clang of armor. When not fighting pitched battles with their neighbors, killing huge lizards with St. George, or thrashing the infidels with King Richard the Lion, medieval cats—kings, jesters, knights and their ladies—ventured out of their keeps to joust, feast, and engage in some chivalrous lovemaking. Their amorous pursuits, unfortunately, exposed another fatal feline flaw—jealousy—as the tragic tale of King Arthur and the Round Table so exquisitely illustrates.

VIKING CATS

FEROCIOUS and as fiery as his red fur,
Eric the Red Cat feared not man nor beast nor raging
seas. Fleeing from Iceland after a nasty spat, Eric
sailed with his hearty Vikings in search of a land
rumored to be somewhere to the west. After many
months of guiding their small wooden ships through
dangerous ice-bound seas, the Viking cats found the
land they were looking for and called it Greenland.
Eric returned to Iceland to gather colonists for his
new land. Most hearth-loving cats were reluctant to
follow Eric to this cold and distant isle, but Eric
enticed them with an irresistible promise:
all the fish they could eat.

AZTEC CATS

HISS-TORY records that the Aztec cats first arrived in Mexico's central plateau around 1000 A.D. where they managed to build one of the world's great civilizations in a swampland. No satisfactory explanation has ever been given for the appearance of this sophisticated community at such a time and place. It has been suggested that the Aztecs were actually inhabitants of another planet possessing advanced technological know-how. The explanation, however, may be more mundane. Given the unique ability of felines to sense energy impulses beyond the immediate surroundings, it seems more likely that the Aztec cats were simply receiving signals from the catmosphere.

SAMURAI CATS

THE BARONIAL cats of feudal Japan (though they were called daiymos) were no different than their European counterparts. Their power depended heavily on the support of well-armed followers, and thus developed in the 12th century the class of cat warriors known as samurai. Samurai cats formed a distinct caste in Japan for over 800 years. As a mark of their distinguished position they, and only they, were permitted to wear two swords and ostentatious armor. They followed a rigid code of ethics known as bushido, and—unlike ordinary cats—were intensely loyal to their daiymo. By the mid-17th century samurai cats had largely laid down their arms, choosing instead to pursue the delights of sushi, kabuki, electronics, small rodents, and birds. It is a curious but little-known fact that samurai always traveled in groups of seven—a mystical number in keeping with the spirit of these enigmatic cats.

CAT COLUMBUS

IT HAS OFTEN been said, by the remarkably uninformed, that cats do not like water. This was certainly not the case with one of hiss-tory's greatest seafarers, Christopher "Cat" Columbus. A native of Italy, Columbus ended up in Lisbon having survived a wreck at sea. After working out elaborate if slightly flawed calculations, he proposed the sensational idea that the Far East could be reached by sailing west. The Portuguese royal maritime commission thought he was mad, so he went next door to Spain and scratched on the door of Queen Isabella until he had reduced it to splinters. With her support he set sail for Asia, never dreaming that his firmly held convictions would lead him to an entirely unknown land mass. It should come as no surprise that a cat was responsible for this earth-shattering discovery, as it was entirely the result of curiosity.

MONA CAT

ONE of the most celebrated portraits ever painted
features a charming feline of unknown name. The
creator, Leonardo Da Vinci, was the true embodiment
of the Renaissance cat, encompassing within his
felinity the skills of artist and engineer as well as the
genius of architect and scientist. Da Vinci so loved
this portrait that he carried it with him everywhere he
went. Over the years a great deal of speculation has
been voiced regarding the subject's mysterious smile.
From certain cryptic notes in Da Vinci's diary recently
deciphered, it is clear that it is almost certainly
related to the disappearance of his favorite canary.

NEW WORLD CATS

SOCIETIES throughout the ages have marked harvest time with festivals of thanksgiving for another year of survival. In recent hiss-tory we find an excellent example of this practice introduced by those hearty individualists, the Pilgrim Cats. Rather than be spiritual slaves to a religion they had no heart for (and only a fool would question the spiritual independence of cats), the Pilgrim Cats had left England for the New World in 1620. Life was not easy on the rocky shores of the New World and when the first harvest was complete, the little colony at Plymouth celebrated with a day of thanksgiving and prayer. They prepared a feast which they shared with the Native American Cats who had helped them in their struggle. Naturally, a large bird was the center of attention.

REVOLUTIONARY CATS

DEFEATED in New York in late summer 1776, the Continental Army, a rag-tag band of intrepid warriors, withdrew across the Delaware River into Pennsylvania to lick their paws and wait for the right moment to avenge their humiliation. Finally, on a bitterly cold Christmas night, the courageous General Washington led his fearless young cats back across the Delaware River into New Jersey and broke up a rousing beer and schnitzel party as well as a few Hessian heads. Washington, as we know, went on to become top cat of the new nation, due in no small part to his knowing when to pounce.

PIONEER CATS

LIGHTING OUT for new territory is nothing new for cats, and the expansion of the United States westward was largely due to their adventurous spirit. On horseback, in wagons, by railroad, and even on paws, they went in search of places where they wouldn't be fenced in. They didn't call it the Wild West for nothing, I can assure you. It was every cat for himself in those early days, and they came up with some ingenious ways to amuse themselves after an exhausting day taming the land, herding the cows, and building the railroads. There is no truth to the popular notion that the West was peppered with saloons selling spirits. As everyone knows, cats deeply dislike even the smell of alcohol, and Miss Kitty served nothing more potent than sarsaparilla dusted with catnip.

LES CHATS

A QUITE EXTRAORDINARY spate of international expositions engulfed all of Europe in the latter half of the 19th century. Given the nature of cat vanity, it is not surprising that large permanent structures were erected to mark these occasions. The first was royal cat Prince Albert's magnificent Crystal Palace for the 1851 London Exposition, where the first international cat show took place a few years later. But it was the 1889 Fourth International Exposition Universelle in Paris that gave the world one of the most enduring national icons, the Eiffel Tower. Designed and built by French feline engineer Alexandre Gustave Eiffel, the 984-foot cast iron tower has stairs, elevators, and three platforms. With the opening of this magnificent monument, it could be said that M. Eiffel, le grand chat, had surely landed on his feet.

KITTY HAWK

CATS, as you know, have been avid bird watchers since the beginning of time and the desire to be airborne no doubt has deep roots in the wish to emulate our feathered friends. It took many centuries before advances in science and engineering allowed the imagination to realize its dream. In 1903 Orville and Wilbur Wright, a couple of creative cats who operated the local bicycle shop,

managed to construct the first flying machine. The 750-pound Kitty Hawk struggled into the air over the dunes of North Carolina's Kill Devil Hills for an incredible 12 seconds. The name of the first airplane is mistakenly believed to refer to the place where this momentous event took place. But I don't think I have to tell you, dear reader, that the name celebrates the moment that cats became birds, if only momentarily.

COOL CATS

THE POSTWAR YEARS saw American culture emerge as the catalyst for a new vitality worldwide. Cool cats were "on the road" in record numbers, jiving to a new beat in music, cruising into the brave new world of an asphalt jungle where the excitement of drive-up snack bars, drive-in movies, and drive-through car washes altered the physical and mental landscape. Crazy cats in black charted unfamiliar territory and, not surprisingly, this new energy found its most famous literary expression in a poem entitled, "Yowl."

43

LUNAR CATS

THE MOON LANDING in July 1969
by three American catronauts offers perhaps the most
dramatic example of how patient planning and rare
vision combined to give us an astonishing moment in
hiss-tory. Eight years of intensive preparation led to
that memorable day when catronaut Armstrong
stepped onto the surface of another planet and
declared: "That's one small step for man,
one giant leap for cats!"

CYBER CATS

.THE EXPLOSIVE growth of technology in the latter half of our present century would not have been possible but for the invention of the computer. It is not often mentioned, but the true genius responsible for developing the basic principles of the digital computer was a delicate female feline by the name of Augusta Ada Byron. The computer, it may thus be said, originated in the union of art and science, as Augusta, a brilliant mathematician, was the daughter of that aristocatic romantic poet, Lord Byron. Together with her associate Charles Babbage, Augusta invented the Analytical Engine in the early years of her royal catness Queen Victoria's reign on which all later computing machines were based. The influence of later cyber cats on the development of computers is evident even in the smallest details. Who else, after all, would have called it a "mouse?"